BEAUTY
FOR
Ashes

SHEENA R. STEELE

Library of Congress Control Number   2021917992
ISBN: Softcover   978-1-950425-43-3
               eBook   978-1-950425-44-0

Published in the United States of America.

Liber Publishing House
www.liberpublishing.com
Hotline: 718 577 1006

Quantity sales. Special discounts are available on quantity purchases by corporations, associations, and others. For details, contact the publisher at above information.

Contents

Running Back to You

I try to get a grasp on You,
Then I fall behind,
I try to get a move on,
The way rock climbers climb,
I want You and I need You so,
I never wanna let You go,
For You're the one I desire,
Just like a raging fire,
You gave Your life for me so many years ago,
I just want to let You know how much I love You so,
You're always there for me in all my pain and strife,
I just want to praise You for the rest of my life,
You're my Rock and my Salvation,
You are my motivation,
To go on each day,
And face the trouble that come my way,
I don't know why you love me so,
In spite of what I do,
You're always thinking of me,
That's why I wanna praise You,
I know I'm not perfect and if I rely on man,
He'll bring me down every time he can,
So I'll just put my trust in You,
The only perfect man who died for all my sins,
Who will always love me until the very end.

Amazing Grace

Disrespected, misused,
Heartbroken, lied to,
In a world with disgrace,
But thank God for His grace,
This world in turmoil,
Cause the devil tried to foil,
God's plan for man,
But God said, "Hey I got a backup plan,"
And sent Jesus to the earth,
To Joseph and Mary,
Through a virgin birth,
He performed miracles and wonders,
For everyone to see,
Had everyone in awe,
Then was crucified on a tree,
And died for you and me,
Then rose on the third day,
With all power in His hand,
And took away the power of Satan,
So I thank God for His love and mercies and grace,
And I am just waiting for the day,
When I finally see his face.

Sheena R. Steele

The Rescue

The day was dark,
The sun was down,
It seemed like no one was around,
This day of sadness,
Too dismayed,
What would come the next day?
People running frantic, not knowing what to do,
Then all of a sudden someone came to the rescue,
He pulled people to safety,
Out of the way of danger,
As he was looking into the eyes of a stranger,
He knew not what to say,
He prayed this day would not last,
Things were moving too fast,
For everything was too crude,
It seemed like a nightmare come true,
All of the people who risked their lives,
Could never forget the fear in their eyes,
All the rescuers were heroes that day,
For they knew that this memory would not go away.

(Dedicated to everyone who risked their lives on
September 11th, 2001)

Restored Soul

You say so many lies,
I don't know when you tell the truth,
I believed you so many times,
It's like stepping off a roof,
I fell for you in an odd type of way,
Then you laughed at me,
And just walked away,
You say you'll do anything for me,
Then do the opposite,
You say you love me so,
Then break all your promises,
I don't know how to love you now,
So I'll just let you go,
Get on your way and get out of my life,
So I can fulfill my soul.

Sheena R. Steele

Breaking The Curse

Black people die,
White people lie,
In the streets,
You're considered a snitch,
If you tell on ya peeps,
And call you a bitch,
Can't tell a good cop,
From a bad cop,
That's how Johnny got shot,
Dead lifeless body,
Cops shooting like a hobby,
Streets filled with blood strains,
Can't comprehend it with your brain,
But you still live with the pain,
Of being stereotyped over and over again,
Johnny's not coming home tonight,
Cause a cop took his life,
One less plate at the dinner table tonight,
Gotta stand up and fight,
For what is right,
Don't get used to it,
All this hate crime,
Going on outside your door,
It's a race war,
Going on,
But some people,
Too scared to admit it,
We gotta stand up and fight somehow,
To hope for a better day,
All we can do is hope and pray,
For peace and justice,
To reign on earth,
Until Jesus comes back,
And breaks the curse.

God's Creations

Eagles soaring high,
Owls howling in the night,
Butterflies' soaring,
Lions roaring,
Beautiful night sky,
Stars twinkling bright,
Nothing to worry about,
Nature is marvelous,
The tide of the ocean,
Flowers bloom,
Mountains stand firm,
While the sky,
Is decorated purple and blue,
God's creations,
In all His glory,
Magnificent and breathtaking,
He is Alpha and Omega,
The Beginning and the End,
Lion of Judah,
The Holy One who is to come,
Til Jesus returns,
I will bask in all Your wonderful, beautiful handiwork.

Sheena R. Steele

Untitled

Too little, too late,
Just another mistake,
Lied to, cheated on,
Just another heartbreak,
So tired of this mess,
I just want some happiness,
Bad boys, thug type,
Kind of guys,
I used to like,
So tired, misused,
My heart you bruised,
Just trying to love you right,
But you're not worth my time,
I'll go my way,
You go the left lane,
Cause you're just a mistake,
I'll never make again,
I gave you my all,
And you let me fall,
Dropped me like a bad habit,
Couldn't answer my call,
My eyes are open,
Now I see,
You were never good for me,
I had to think twice,
Maybe I was too nice,
Too naïve to see,
What you were doing to me,
But now my heart is open,
For the one I deserve,
To love me the way,
You never could.

My God

God is my peace,
My stronghold, my hope,
My strong tower,
He gives me peace that showers,
All over me,
Making me feel light as a feather,
As sweet smelling as a flower,
He gives me beauty for ashes, joy for my sadness,
His love is forever,
Makes me happy to be in His presence,
He makes me wanna sing, makes me wanna dance,
Lift up holy hand,
Over and over again,
The Alpha and Omega,
Beginning and End,
Author of my faith,
Faith that never ends,
His love envelopes me,
Makes me whole,
He covers and protects me,
Never lets me go,
He is the Promise keeper,
His word is bond,
I know when I am weak,
That's when He is strong.

Sheena R. Steele

Real Love

What I thought was real love,
Was just silly crush,
I thought he was the one for me,
Til I looked up above,
Beyond the heavens and the stars,
A real love waited for me,
Coming down from the clouds,
A love so fantastic,
I never want to come down,
A love so incredible,
This I now can see,
God looked beyond all my faults,
To see me for me,
He took me under His wing,
And guided me along the path,
To a journey focused on my future,
Rather than my past.

My Happiness

My happiness is the center of my joy,
It comes from within my soul,
I have a forever flowing peace within me,
Like a flowing serenity,
When I get happy,
I can shout and sing and dance,
I love to sing praises,
And lift up holy hands,
To praise the One who made me,
In His image and creativity,
My freedom to praise my God,
Is more than I can bear,
Cause even I praise Him,
It's my choice, do or dare,
I'm as free as a bird,
It's my choice to praise my God,
Any way I want,
Whether it's through laughter, song, or dance,
It's my time, now is my chance.

Sheena R. Steele

All-Star

The world is coming to an end,
Yet so many people fail to see it,
Trying to copy the latest trends,
Caught up in your own little worlds,
Doing enough just to get by,
When this day could be your last try,
To get your life straight with God,
Cause He's coming like a thief in the night,
There ain't no alarm clock,
To wake you when it's through,
If God doesn't know you,
Then you need some praying to do,
He doesn't care what time you wanna die,
When this very night,
Could be your last goodbye,
So you'd better stop trying to front,
Like you all hard,
Cause compared to God,
He's the only all-star,
He made the heavens and the earth,
He was even nailed to a tree,
And died for you and me,
So now you know the truth,
You ain't the baddest one around,
The only one worthy to be praised,
Is God, the baddest cat in town!

Healed Heart

You give your all,
To have your heart broken,
Your heart ripped out, stomped on like a token,
Like someone ripped your heart out and threw it out the door,
Then stomped it all over the floor,
One of the worst feelings you will ever know,
But slowly and surely, you learn to let go,
To let God heal,
Get back your zeal,
God mends your heart back together again,
Making it whole again,
So you can have the courage to love fully,
Without having to worry,
About being hurt again,
Because your heart He already did mend,
So you can give your love to the one who deserves it,
The one God chose for you because He knew you were
worth it.

Angel In Disguise

An angel among us,
Though we didn't even know,
When you left,
How it hurt you so,
The pain you felt,
How it hurt you so,
You're free now,
It's okay to let go,
Now you're in a better place,
Full of happiness and grace,
You mounted up with wings,
As you said I'm finally free,
Out of life's debt,
Now you can rest,
You touched our hearts,
With your serenity and grace,
Now you're in heaven,
With God shining upon your face,
You taught us a lesson,
We would never forget,
Now you're in heaven,
Fully out of life's debt.

Hated For Who I Am

You can hate me for who I am,
But you ain't gonna stop me,
From doing what's right,
Trying to fulfill God's prophesy,

I got haters all over me,
Just waiting for me to fall,
I can't afford to stumble,
Gotta give the Lord my all,

See, I ain't gonna change,
Just so you can like me,
I'd rather be hated for who I am,
Than loved to not be,

So you can go ahead,
And talk about me for all I care,
I'd rather represent the One,
For all my sins He had to bare.

Home

One lonely night,
Just sitting, thinking,
Of everything I could've been,
Of all the couldas, shouldas and wouldas been,
Then I remember who I am and whose I am,
A daughter of the Most High God,
He encourages me, pushes me on,
When I want to give in,
He's never left my side and never will,
He lifts me up when I've sunken down deep in despair,
And reminds me I'm the apple of His eye,
He will never leave or forsake me,
He loves me through it all,
Forevermore, that's who I am,
A Child of God, a daughter in Christ Jesus,
And I don't have to look anywhere else for acceptance,
Because I am home forevermore.

Love Back

She had a weak moment,
He came into her life,
And turned it upside down,
She fell in love head over heels,
He used her up and left her,
Left her to deal with all the pain,
Her heart was broken,
She felt like it broke in a million pieces,
As she tried to pick up the pieces,
He slowly came back into her life,
She didn't know what to do,
For he had a piece of her heart,
She could not get back,
She couldn't stand to get hurt again,
She grabbed all the faith and dignity she had and let him go,
For her self-worth and self-respect was priceless,
She finally realized that and loved herself.

Sheena R. Steele

My Sweet Pea

My precious baby boy,
Heaven blessed me with such joy,
To have you in my life,
When I look into your eyes,
Everything seems just right,
Just to see your smile,
And hear your laughter,
Nothing else matters,
So busy, jumping and running and playing,
I love it when to my arms he lays in,
He gives the best hugs and kisses,
And when he's away,
Oh, how I miss it,
He's an energized ball of joy,
He's my sweet little baby boy.

The Joy I Found,

You may think you get the best of me,
When you talk about me constantly,
Always trying to belittle me,
Like you're better than me,
Talking about my clothes, my style, my hair,
Nothing can compare,
To the way you act when you walk into a room,
Trying to intimidate me, yet you still assume,
That you're better than me,
Cause you have the latest trends,
The latest hairstyle and clothes,
But I suppose,
You're just trying to get attention,
Cause that's all that you can do,
Trying to have the latest in everything,
Try walking in my shoes,
Then maybe you'll see,
What you have is not everything,
See I don't care what you say,
The lies you tell about me every day,
Because I know who I am,
I'm a woman of God,
He loves and protects me,
At all costs,
He keeps me in peace and keeps me happy,
I don't have to worry, I don't have to stress,
I have the joy of the Lord,
I know I'll pass the test.

Sheena R. Steele

Untitled VI

Another lifeless body in the street,
Killed by a white man claiming,
"It wasn't me,"
He looks "suspicious",
So he looks for his gun,
So he could kill another one,
An innocent black man,
Whose life was taken,
Stolen by a racist,
Did he do it for show,
You know the answer to that,
Everyone knows,
Blood on the pavement,
From the gunshot wound,
When will they learn not to assume,
That just because his skin is different,
It doesn't mean better or worse,
It's just different,
Now Andre's in a hearse,
We're all human, running the same race,
We all bleed the same,
So don't look at us different,
Just thank God for His grace.

Blindness

Once I was blind,
To the darkness that surrounded me,
I had the light within me,
But I failed to see what it was meant to be,
All my family and friends,
Told me you were no good,
But I had to find out for myself,
Unfortunately, you helped,
You led me on,
When you didn't even like me,
You pretended to, to get what you could,
My mam always said you were no good,
You lied to me,
Used me consistently,
To get what you wanted,
Til you got sick of me,
You didn't care,
When I cried my eyes out,
You knew that I loved you,
Then tore my heart apart,
You knew that I loved you,
And used it to your advantage,
To break my heart,

Sheena R. Steele

How could you be so harsh,
You saw the right through me,
I knew what you did,
But I was so in love,
So my intelligence I hid,
All the heartache, hurt and pain,
You put me through,
But you didn't care,
Cause it didn't concern you,
I loved you and hated you,
All at the same time,
But you never loved me,
You kept telling me lies,
You never loved me,
The way I wanted you to,
I now know you just wanted to go,
I later realized,
You were never goof for me,
Like a rotten apple,
It's too late to eat,
Cause that fruit on the table,
It was never meant to be.

Floating On Air

A love so fantastic,
It's almost like magic,
Just like in a fairy tale,
Caught up in a love spell,
I dream about it,
And wish I was there,
Cause I know love is in the air,
Flying on high,
Soaring through the skies,
Riding on the clouds,
As they rise higher in the sky,
I'm soaring like an eagle,
Just like I can fly,
As I ascend,
To the highest of heights,
I'm lost in eternal bliss,
Only thinking of that one kiss,
I'm drunk on your love,
Cause I'm the only one you're thinking of.

Sheena R. Steele

She Still Loved Him

She was so gullible,
He came into her life,
Like a thief in the night,
And turned her world upside down,
She felt like she was drowning,
She was stunned,
Because she fell for him so fast,
But now she was his past,
But that wasn't the end,
Because she was pregnant,
Her whole life changed,
It would never be the same,
Then suddenly the guy disappeared,
Without a word whispered,
She was breathless,
Taken aback,
He slowly came into her life,
Then was gone before the break of light,
She could not forget him,
For she still loved him,
Now she has a son,
Her new life has just begun,
But she still remembers her first love,
Even through all the pain he put her through,
And how he manipulated her so,
But she still loved him.

My Future Husband

I can't wait,
For the man of my dreams,
The one who I'll meet,
Who'll sweep me off my feet,
The one who God created, just for me,
He'll love and adore me,
Be a man of God,
After His own heart,
He'll love my heart,
And never tear it apart,
My husband will love and respect me,
Never neglect me,
We'll live life together,
In harmony forever,
Having the best time,
Until Jesus calls us home,
Forever in His arms.

The One Who Holds My Future

I never felt this way before,
My life is like an open door,
For God to manifest,
Bring to pass,
The things You see in me best,
My future is bright,
Like someone turned on,
A bright light,
I listen when You speak,
Or I'll miss the message,
And be bleak,
I obey Your word O Lord,
For You are the One I adore,
O how I love You so,
I never wanna let go,
Of Your faithful hand,
You let me know,
Your love is so true,
Time and time again,
Like the calmness of the sea,
You bring out the best in me,
You hold my hand,
And never let go,
You're so patient and kind,
Faithful and true,
All I wanna do is love like You do.

Real Friends

What I want to know,
Why some friends leave,
While others stay,
The ones who leave,
Have nothing nice to say,
They talk behind your back,
Then claim to have your back,
All the while they're laughing behind you,
Plotting your downfall,
Hoping you fall,
Like standing on a log,
Maybe it's all part of God's plan,
To choose your friends wisely,
Get your head out the clouds,
And learn a lesson,
From the One holding the pen,
Who's writing your story,
So don't fret, don't worry,
Cause people come and go,
Some stay for life,
Others stay for show,
Some stay for a season,
Others stay for the right reason,
The real friends stay,
For the best reasons,
They'll never leave,
They stay 'til the end,
Some friends betray you,
Lead you astray,
While others, your real friends,
Will never turn away.

Sheena R. Steele

Worst Enemies

You smile at me and talk to me,
Like you really care,
Then talk about me,
When I'm not even there,
Like a fragile glass,
You're afraid it might break,
It's too late!
I caught on to you,
All the things you put me through,
You took advantage of me,
I let you, so what's new?
You knew I would do anything for you,
But now you've lost your only true friend,
What are you going to do?
Try looking at the mirror,
And finding what you see,
That the person looking back,
Is your own worst enemy.

Soul Cry

Praying for You to guide,
To keep me strong,
And help me carry on,
Through these tough times,
And show me a sign,
To help lead and guide me,
In all my ways,
Lord give me the strength,
To lift up Your name,
And walk in a treacherous world,
Full of deceit and sins,
To live this life confident in You,
That You will see me through,
Until the very end.

Sheena R. Steele

Coming Home

This feeling of restlessness,
Of what I should do,
Do what I hate,
Hate what I do,
Do what is right,
Or deny what I know is true,
I know what to do,
The right thing is true,
But it's hard sometimes,
To resist,
What I want to do,
I know it's wrong,
But the feeling gets so strong,
Then I'm reminded,
To whom I belong,
I can do all things,
To him who believes,
I have the strength,
To resist the temptation,
The devil has to flee,
I know I can achieve,
Everything I was meant to,
It's because of what I believe,
Because He lives inside of me,
Cause greater is He,
Who lives inside me,

Than he that is in the world,
I once thought I couldn't ignore,
The temptation that keeps,
Knocking at my door,
But now I know,
God is all I need,
To survive and make a better life for me,
Cause Lord knows I need His help,
Every day of my life,
He loves and protects me,
And heals me by His stripes,
He's the lover of my soul,
It's to Jesus I can go,
He comforts me with His loving embrace,
And mercies and grace,
He helps me to win this race,
In Him I live, move and have my being,
Jesus, my Lord, my Savior, my King,
Every second, every minute, every hour of the day,
Lord, I need You,
I cannot wait,
So please, have mercy on me,
I can't do it alone,
I need You now, Lord,
I wanna come home.

Sheena R. Steele

The End Times

These are the end times,
And if you ain't with it,
You gonna miss it,
Thinking you still got another day,
To sit around and play,
This ain't a time to play,
To hang with your crew,
With nothing left to do,
Thinking every day,
Is promised to you,
There's a holy war going on,
This ain't a time for fun,
It's the end times,
And as you can see,
If you read the scriptures,
Of the Bible, it'll getcha,
Convict ya, because,
There are wars and rumor of wars,
How much more evidence can you afford?
There are diseases,
All kinds of seizures,
Famines and droughts,

Do you know what I'm talking about?
COVID-19 all over the place,
And if you ain't careful,
It'll hit you in the face,
Could it be one of the seven plagues,
That's mentioned in the Bible?
If this is so,
Then it makes us more liable,
To do the things,
The Bible mentions,
In these times,
People don't care what they're missing,
Thinking they all hard,
Cursing, then try to be churchin',
You need to stop,
Get on your knees and pray,
So you can get right with God,
In each and every way,
So before I end my rhymes,
You need to recognize,
That we are living in the end times.

Grandma (R.I.P.)

She was a kind, caring soul,
With a heart full of gold,
Unafraid to speak her mind,
To keep you in line,
Had a switch,
She would grab,
With a flick of her wrist,
To do what she had,
If you act bad,
Wore her heart on her sleeve,
Would do anything to help you achieve,
All of your dreams,
Everything that you see,
A hardworking woman of God,
Would do any odd job,
She had an infectious smile,
That would keep you smiling for miles and miles,
Oh, and that laugh,
Could make you just laugh,
For miles and miles,
Her caring nature,
Never went out of style,
I loved you then,
And I love you still,
Til we meet again in Heaven,
I know that I will.

9 781950 425433